W9-AAS-752

HORSE — 30 MILES (48 KM) PER HOUR

SKATEBOARD — 15 MILES (24 KM) PER HOUR

DOG — 20 MILES (32 KM) PER HOUR

BULLET TRAIN — 165 MILES (266 KM) PER HOUR

NOW THAT'S FAST!: BULLET TRAINS

JACKRABBIT — 45 MILES (72 KM) PER HOUR

HUMAN — 12 MILES (19 KM) PER HOUR

BICYCLE — 15 MILES (24 KM) PER HOUR

NOW **THAT'S FAST!**

BULLET TRAINS

KATE RIGGS

CREATIVE EDUCATION

J385
R16

Published by Creative Education
P.O. Box 227, Mankato, Minnesota 56002
Creative Education is an imprint of
The Creative Company
www.thecreativecompany.us

Book and cover design by Blue Design
(www.bluedes.com)
Art direction by Rita Marshall
Printed in the United States of America

Photographs by Alamy (Picture), Corbis (Jose
Fuste Raga/zefa), Getty Images (AFP, DAJ,
Michael Dunning, Yasuhide Fumoto, Rory
Gordon-Michael Ramage, Justin Guariglia,
TEH ENG KOON/AFP, MASATO TOKIWA/A.
Collection, Pete Turner, PIERRE VERDY/AFP),
iStockphoto (Denise Roup)

Copyright © 2010 Creative Education
International copyright reserved in all
countries. No part of this book may be
reproduced in any form without written
permission from the publisher.

Library of Congress Cataloging-in-
Publication Data
Riggs, Kate.
Bullet trains / by Kate Riggs.
p. cm. — (Now that's fast!)
Includes index.
Summary: A quick-paced, colorful
description of the physical characteristics,
purposes, early history, and high-speed
capabilities of bullet trains—the fastest
passenger trains in the world.
ISBN 978-1-58341-911-3
1. High speed trains—Juvenile literature.
I. Title. II. Series.

TF1455.R54 2010
385—dc22
          009002750

First Edition
9 8 7 6 5 4 3 2 1

A bullet train is a high-speed **passenger** train. Bullet trains are the fastest trains in the world. Most bullet trains can go more than 150 miles (241 km) per hour.

Sometimes bridges are built to help bullet trains go straight

Bullet trains are used to carry people from place to place. Some bullet trains carry **freight**, too. Most bullet trains run on electricity. But some use diesel (*DEE-suhl*) gasoline like regular trains.

All bullet trains have parts called **locomotives**. They are on each end of the train. A locomotive has a pointed nose like the front of an airplane. Between the two locomotives are train cars. The longest trains have 16 to 18 cars.

10

People board, or get on, a bullet train when it stops at a station

Bullet trains run on special railroad tracks. The tracks are straight and smooth. A person called a conductor drives the bullet train.

A conductor sits in a small space in the front of the locomotive

People in Japan rode the first bullet train in 1964. It ran between the cities of Tokyo and Osaka. The train was called the Shinkansen (*shin-KAHN-sen*). Soon, people in Europe (*YOO-rup*) built fast trains, too.

The big nose of the Shinkansen gave bullet trains their name

French bullet trains are part of the railway company SNCF

Most bullet trains are still in Japan. They can go almost 200 miles (322 km) per hour! France has a bullet train called the TGV. Spain has a bullet train called the AVE.

A TGV train called the Eurostar goes between France and England. There is a lot of water between France and England. The Eurostar goes through a tunnel under the water. The tunnel connects the two countries.

18

Eurostar trains start at a station in the city of London, England

When a bullet train zooms
along the smooth tracks, it
can be hard to see. It goes so
fast that it is a blur. It does not
stop until it reaches a station.

Bullet trains are built to be strong and
to move smoothly along the tracks

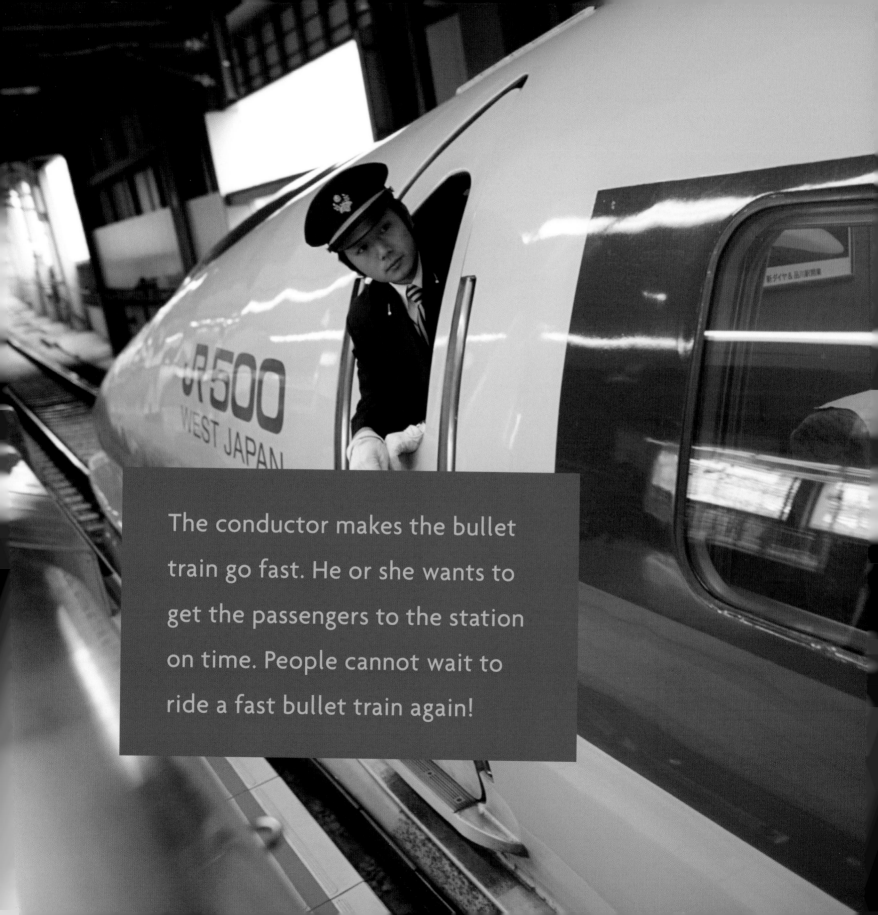

The conductor makes the bullet train go fast. He or she wants to get the passengers to the station on time. People cannot wait to ride a fast bullet train again!

Fast Facts

California plans to build a bullet train to connect the cities of San Francisco and Los Angeles.

Some AVE trains are nicknamed "Ducks" because the front of the train looks like a duck's beak.

A train in China goes 217 miles (350 km) per hour every day. It is the fastest train in daily use.

A bullet train in France set a speed record in 2007. It went 357 miles (575 km) per hour!

Glossary

freight—things that are carried on a train, like mail from a post office

locomotives—the first cars on a train that pull the other cars behind them

passenger—someone who rides on a train or other vehicle

record—something that is the best or most ever

Read More about It

Balkwill, Richard. *The Best Book of Trains*. New York: Kingfisher, 1999.

Hofer, Charles. *Bullet Trains*. New York: PowerKids Press/Rosen Publishing Group, 2008.

Web Site

Kids Web Japan: Bullet Train
http://web-japan.org/kidsweb/hitech/shinkansen/index.html
This site explores the Japanese Shinkansen bullet trains.

Index